The Crocodiles And Lizards Of Borneo In
The Sarawak Museum: With Descriptions Of
Supposed New Species

Edward Bartlett

In the interest of creating a more extensive selection of rare historical book reprints, we have chosen to reproduce this title even though it may possibly have occasional imperfections such as missing and blurred pages, missing text, poor pictures, markings, dark backgrounds and other reproduction issues beyond our control. Because this work is culturally important, we have made it available as a part of our commitment to protecting, preserving and promoting the world's literature. Thank you for your understanding.

THE CROCODILES AND LIZARDS OF BORNEO
IN THE SARAWAK MUSEUM,

WITH

DESCRIPTIONS OF SUPPOSED NEW SPECIES,

AND

THE VARIATION OF COLOURS IN THE SEVERAL SPECIES DURING LIFE.

By EDWARD BARTLETT,

Curator of the Sarawak Museum.

APRIL, 1894.

Lizards at all times are lively, harmless and interesting reptiles, their movements are graceful and smooth, in some genera, while others are rather uncouth, but all have that cunning quick attractive eye which calls one's attention to them at once.

There is no doubt that a large proportion of the lizards are more or less chameleon-like as regards the habit of changing colour, but at the same time there are many whose colours are permanent or attained during the breeding season; and these permanent colours are assumed by gradual development and age.

If ornithologists are justified in making three species of *Halcyon torquatus*, *H. fortesi*, and *H. molimbicus*, on such slender variations,* I consider that where we find a considerable number of different constant (permanent) colours in these lizards we are equally entitled to treat them as separate species.

---

* To quote another instance of species differing in colour only—and that to a trivial extent—it becomes a question in my mind whether it is age or sex that causes the distinction between *Eurystomus orientalis* and *E. calonyx*, the two species being found together.

The number of species of lizards found in Borneo, is not very great considering the size of the island, viz.:—

1 Crocodile.

1 Gavial.

61 Lizards, two of which are doubtful Bornean species, viz., *Tarentola Delalandii*, and *Mabuia Delalandii*.

To facilitate quick reference, I have retained Mr. Boulenger's nomenclature of the species; each species will be found with a reference to the pages of the three volumes:

Catalogue of Chelonians, 1889.
Catalogue of Lizards, 1885-7.

Those marked S. M. are in the Sarawak Museum.

Nominal List of the Crocodiles and Lizards of Borneo.

1. Crocodilus porosus, Müll.
2. Tomistoma Schlegelii, Müll.
3. Gymnodactylus marmoratus, Kuhl.
4.   ,, consobrinus, Ptrs.
5. Gonatodes Kendallii, Gray.
6.   ,, ornatus, Bedd.
7. Œlurosaurus felinus, Gthr.
8.   ,, dorsalis, Ptrs.
9. Hemidactylus frenatus, D. & B.
10.   ,, Brookei, Gray.
11.   ,, platyurus, Schn.
12. Gehyra mutilata, Wiegm.
13. Lepidodactylus aurantiacus, Bedd.
14. Gecko verticillatus, Laur.
15.   ,, stentor, Cant.
16.   ,, monarchus, D. & B.
17. Ptychozoon homalocephalum, Crev.
18.   ,, Horsfieldii, Gray.
19. Tarentola Delalandii, D. & B.
20. Draco volans, Linn.
21.   ,, cornutus, Gthr.
22.   ,, affinis, n. sp.
23.   ,, rostratus, Gthr.

24. Draco fimbriatus, Kuhl.
25. ,, cristatellus, Gthr.
26. ,, hæmatopogan, Gray.
27. ,, tæniopterus, Gthr.
28. ,, quinquefasciatus, Gray.
29. ,, maximus, Blgr.
30. ,, microlepis, Blgr.
31. ,, nigriappendiculatus, n. sp.
32. ,, grandis, n. sp.
33. Aphaniotis fusca, Ptrs.
34. Gonyocephalus doriæ, Ptrs.
35. ,, liogastor, Gthr.
36. ,, miotympanum, Gthr.
37. ,, borneensis, Schleg.
38. ,, grandis, Gray.
39. Japalura nigrilabris, Ptrs.
40. Calotes cristatellus, Kuhl.
41. Lanthanotus borneensis, Stdchr.
42. Varanus Dumeritii, Schleg.
43. ,, heteropholis, Blgr.
44. ,, rudicollis, Gray.
45. ,, salvator, Laur.
46. Tachydromus sexlineatus, Daub.
47. Mabuia Delalandii, D. & B.
48. ,, rugifera, Stol.
49. ,, rubricollis, n. sp.
50. ,, multifasciata, Kuhl.
51. ,, rudis, Blgr.
52. ,, kuchingensis, n. sp.
53. ,, Lewisi, n. sp.
54. ,, saravacensis n. sp.
55. Lygosoma variegatum, Ptrs.
56. ,, kinabaluensis, n. sp.
57. ,, olivaceum, Gray.
58. ,, vittatum, Edel.
59. ,, nitens, Ptrs.
60. ,, parietale, Ptrs.
61. Lygosoma (Kiopa) Bampfyldei, n. sp.
62. Tropidophorus Beccari, Ptrs.
63. ,, Brookei, Gray.

1.—*Crocodilus porosus*, Boulen. Cat. Chelon., p. 284, 1889.

Schneider's crocodile. Buâia of the Malays. S. M.

The crocodile is plentiful along the sea coast, and in all the rivers of Borneo. It attains a great length in this country, and also becomes very robust. One specimen in this Museum from the Baram river, obtained by Mr. C. Hose measures over 17 feet.

Sarawak river *(E. Bartlett)*; Baram River *(C. Hose)*.

Another species is reported to exist in some parts of the country, which I presume must be *Crocodilus palustris*, by the description of it, viz.:— "that the head is much longer and narrower," but up to the present moment I have not discovered any difference in the series we have in the Museum.

Many instances of its ferocious habits are reported from time to time; it generally catches bathers who are unaware of its presence. One curious rescue of three little children occurred some time ago; it appears that they were bathing together when a crocodile seized one of them; one got hold of its legs while the other, a little girl, got on top of its head and gouged its eyes until the brute released the other; they were all saved.

2.—*Tomistoma Schlegelii*, Boulen., Cat. Chelon., p. 276, 1889.

Schlegel's Gavial. Buaia sniulong of the Malays. S. M.

This gavial is, from all I can gather, restricted to the estuary and Sadong river. The two specimens in the Museum were brought down alive, having been caught by the Malays with the *ah-lir* cross bar.

Length 11 feet.

Skull of the largest 2 feet 6½ in., width across base 14½ inches.

Sadong estuary and river *(E. Bartlett and Phillips)*; Mulla *(G. Barlow)*.

3.—*Gymnodactylus marmoratus*, Boulen., Cat. Lizards, vol. i, p. 44, 1885.

A single example is in the collection.

Sarawak *(Doria and Beccari)*; Mount Dulit *(C. Hose)*; Kuching *(E. Bartlett)*.

4.— *Gymnodactylus consobrinus*, Boulen., Cat. Lizards, vol. i, p. 47, 1887. S. M.

A single example is in the collection.

Sarawak *(Doria and Beccari)*; Belaga river, Rejang *(C. A. Bampfylde)*.

5.—Gonatodes Kendallii, Boulen., Cat. Lizards, vol. i,
p. 63, 1885, S. M.

Lately obtained near here.

Matang, Sarawak *(G. A. Boulenger)*. Sarawak *(H. Low)*, Kuching *(E. Bartlett)*.

6.—Gonatodes ornatus, Boulen., Cat. Lizards, vol. i,
p. 67, 1885. S. M.

General colour above grass-green marbled all over with brown; a black line from hind corner of eyes to occiput, but not confluent; a black oblong spot occupies the centre; three black spots in front of the shoulder and three behind; six black dorsal spots or streaks; under-parts yellowish green; with a pale purple patch on the throat and another on the middle of the belly.

7.—Œlurosaurus felinus, Boulen., Cat. Lizards, vol. i,
p. 73. 1885. S. M.

Borneo *(Wallace)*.
Penkalan Ampat, Sarawak *(Dr. G. D. Haviland)*.

8.—Œlurosaurus dorsalis, Boulen., Cat. Lizards, vol. i,
p. 74, 1885.

Sarawak *(Doria and Beccari)*

9.—Hemidactylus frenatus, Boulen., Cat. Lizards, vol. i,
p. 120, 1885, S. M.

Not common; frequents houses.
Borneo *(E. Belcher)*; Kuching, Sarawak *(E. Bartlett)*.

10.—Hemidactylus Brookei, Boulen., Cat. Lizards, vol. i,
p. 128, 1885. S. M.

Probably introduced years ago.
Borneo *(E. Belcher)*; Sarawak *(H. Low)*; Kuching *(E. Bartlett)*.

11.—Hemidactylus platyurus, Boulen., Cat. Lizards, vol. i,
p. 143, 1885. S. M.

Not often met with; frequents houses.

Borneo *(E. Belcher and Cantor)*; Sarawak *(Doria and Beccari)*; Kuching, Sarawak *(E. Bartlett)*; Sarawak *(H. Low)*.

12—Gehyra mutilata, Boulen., Cat. Lizards, vol. i,
p. 148, 1885. S. M.

Not uncommon in houses.
Kuching and Banting *(E. Bartlett)*.

13.—Lepidodactylus aurantiacus, (?) Boulen., Cat. Lizards,
vol. i, p. 164, 1885. S. M.

Very rare.
Sautubong *(E. Bartlett)*.

14.—Gecko verticillatus, Boulen., Cat. Lizards, vol. i,
p. 183, 1885. S. M.

Very scarce.
Rejang River, Sarawak *(C. A. Bampfylde)*.

15.—Gecko stentor, Boulen., Cat. Lizards, vol. i, p. 184. S. M.

Singed with pale green all over; eye bright grass green.

This gecko is not abundant, it inhabits hollows in old trees and houses, it is a great annoyance at night on account of the horrible sepulchral noise it makes.

Banjermassing *(Blecker)*; Labuan *(Collingwood)*; Kuching, Sarawak *(E. Bartlett)*; Mount Dulit *(C Hose)*; Kejang river *(C. A. Bampfylde and Leys)*; Undup *(W. Howell)*.

16.—Gecko monarchus, Boulen., Cat. Lizards, vol. i,
p. 187, 1885. S. M.

Chichak of the Malays.

Very abundant throughout all the places which I have visited; in every house and bungalow, also on the barks of trees which are exposed; but not a jungle gecko. The colour varies from dark dirty brown to almost pure white; the black markings or marbling is very intense in some individuals, while in others it is very faint.

Borneo (*E. Belcher, Cantor, and Dillwyn*); Matang (*E Bartlett and Boulenger*); Sarawak (*Doria and Beccari*); Undup (*W. Howell*); Kuching, Sarawak (*E. Bartlett and G. D. Haviland*); Mount Dulit (*C. Hose*).

17.—*Ptychozoon homalocephalum*, Boulen., Cat. Lizards, vol. i. p. 190, 1885. S. M.

Comparatively rare in the Kuching district.

Borneo (*L. L. Dillwyn*); Sarawak (*Doria and Beccari*); Barang, Sarawak (*G. D. Haviland*); Kuching, Sarawak (*E. Bartlett*).

18.—*Ptychozoon Horsfieldii*, Boulen., P. J. S., 1892, p. 505.

I have not seen this species yet, which is no doubt rare.
Mount Dulit (*C. Hose*).

19.—*Tarentola Delalandii*, Boulen., Cat. Lizards, vol. i, p. 199, 1885.

Tarentola borneensis, Gray, Cat., p. 165.

A doubtful Bornean species.

Borneo (*E. Belcher*); Sarawak (*H. Low*).

I find in Mr. Boulenger's catalogue an entry "r.—s. Ad.——? Sir. E. Belcher (P.), (Types of *Tarentola borneensis*);" and Mr. H. Low, also gives this species in his list of Lizards in the appendix (p. 112) to his "Sarawak; its Inhabitants and Productions," 1848. It is highly probable that Sir E. Belcher procured his specimens from the same source, when he visited Borneo; at the same time Mr. H. Low gave specimens to the British Museum, which are not mentioned in the catalogue.

20.—*Draco volans*, Boulen., Cat. Lizards, vol. i, p. 256, 1885. S. M.

Adult male.—Above greyish white marbled and freckled with black; crown of head and orbits bluish-green; wing-menbranes above marbled with brick-red and yellowish green; under surface pale blue; gular appendage bright yellow, very long.

Adult female.—Gular appendage short and dull blue.

Sarawak (*Doria and Beccari*); Borneo (*E. Belcher, Cantor, and R. T. Lowe*); Kuching, Sarawak (*E. Bartlett*).

Very abundant on the trunks of trees on the roadsides throughout the district of Kuching; on very hot days they can be seen darting from tree to tree, with lightning-like rapidity.

21.—Draco cornutus, Boulen., Cat. Lizards, vol. ii. p. 258, 1885. S. M.

Tarang burong of the Malays.

1. *Adult male.*—Upper surface of body bright grass green, varied with black, the green forming five distinct bands across the back; interorbital spot, black enclosed in a pale green circle; nuchal spot, another on lower part of neck and one on each side of it, before the shoulder, black; wing-membrane deep red, spotted and streaked with black, margins black, tinged with green and grey; sides of lower jaw and chin with three or four irregular pale green bands; chest under surface of limbs and belly greyish blue; under surface of wing-membranes brick-red tinged with blue, spotted and streaked with black, these black markings are opposed to those on the upper surface; gular appendage yellowish orange, base bluish.

2. *Adult male.*—Whole of back variegated with bright grass green; wing-membranes black; under parts blue; gular appendage bright salmon-red, edges paler, base bluish.

This very beautiful winged lizard is not a common species in this district. I procured a fine male on Matang at 800 ft.

It is the brightest coloured of all the species found here.

Borneo *(E. Belcher)*; Kuching and Matang *(E. Bartlett)*.

22.—Draco affinis, n. sp., S. M.

Similar to *D. cornutus*, but without the large spine-like scale above the eye. Gular appendage very small; in the female it is almost absent.

Male.—Back dull brown, tinged with green; three distinct greyish white transverse bands on the back; wing membranes above, bright brick red spotted with black, with broad black outer margins, a pale bluish grey line down the centre of the belly; under side of wing membrane dull brick red tinged with blue, and spotted with blackish brown, margined with blotches of black and greyish white.

Adult female.—Back grey mottled with dark brown and tinged with green; wing-membranes bronze green spotted with black, with a broad black band on the outer margin; gular appendage small, yellowish green; chest blue; a line down the centre of belly and under part of hind limbs pale blue, sides of body greyish white mottled with black, underside of wing-membrane yellowish green, outer margin blue.

23.—Draco rostratus, Boulen., Cat. Lizards, vol. i, p. 261, 1885.

Borneo (*E. Belcher*).

24.—Draco fimbriatus, Boulen. Cat. Lizards, vol. i, p. 265, 1885. S. M.

Very rare in this district.
Sarawak (*E. Bartlett*).

25.—Draco cristatellus, Boulen.,. Cat. Lizards, vol. 1, p. 266, 1885. S. M.

Male.—Above grey tinged with brown and black dotted all over; a black interorbital spot; nuchal crest reddish brown; wing-membranes blackish-brown, with a series of longitudinal streaks of yellowish scales; chin grey tinged with green and dotted; gular appendage nearly white; beneath lateral wattles bright buttercup yellow, with a black hind margin to same; belly pale green; under surface of wing-membranes pale blue tinged with yellow.

Not abundant here.
Kuching, Sarawak (*E. Bartlett*).

26.—Draco hæmatopogan, Boulen., Cat. Lizards, vol. i, p. 267, 1885. S. M.

Kuching, Sarawak *(E. Bartlett)*.

27.—Draco tæniopterus, Boulen. Cat. Lizards, vol. i, p. 269, 1885. S. M.

I found this scarce species on Matang at 800 to 900 ft., in June, 1893.

Sarawak (*Doria and Beccari*); Matang, Sarawak (*E. Bartlett*).

28.—*Draco quinquefasciatus*, Boulen., Cat. Lizards, vol. i, p. 267, 1885. S. M.

Male.—General colour above reddish or dirty brown dotted all over, and tinged with bright grass-green over the other colours, it also extends round the margin of the wing-membranes and on all the longitudinal curved lines and ribs, forming rows of green scales; five broad dark brown bands extend across the body and wing-membranes, the broad interspaces are brick-red; a single brown band across the shoulders; under surface of wing-membranes dull yellowish green, crossed by three narrow black bands; body greyish flesh colour; chin greenish; gular and lateral appendages bright yellow, striated with bluish-green, base black; iris golden.

Female.—Resembles the male in all the markings, which are paler and broader, the light grass-green scales are intermixed with scattered white ones, especially on the sides of the head, neck, wing-membranes, and base of tail; a double brown band on the shoulders; under surface like the male; gular and lateral appendages blackish grey faintly striated with greenish white, a yellow spot in the centre of the latter and a blackish stripe on its base.

Rather plentiful about the jungle near Kuching.

Sarawak (*Doria* and *Beccari*); Kuching, Sarawak (*E. Bartlett*); Mount Dulit (*C. Hose*).

29.—*Draco maximus*, Boulen., P. Z. S., 1893, p. 522.

Mount Dulit (*C. Hose*).

30.—*Draco microlepis*, Boulen., P. Z. S., 1893, p. 523.

Merabah, North Borneo (*A. Everett*).

31.—*Draco nigriappendiculatus*, n. sp. S. M.

Habit slender; much more so than *D. volans*; head very small, snout short; nostrils vertical directed upwards; tympanum naked, very small; all the scales above nearly equal, round, and very small; six elongated keeled scales between the nostrils in a line directed backwards; two series of small elongated scales on crown of head forming two stars; a few sharp edged scales in front of the eye; six sets of enlarged scales, three on each side of body; gular appendage long and narrow covered with large flat scales; scales on under parts all keeled and sharp pointed; a few sharp pointed scales along sides of base of tail; tail covered with keeled scales with many fine points.

Male.—Above reddish-buff, marbled with pale brown, and tinged all over with grass green; a small interorbital black spot; three sharp pointed white lateral scales on the sides near the hind legs; wing-membranes nearly black, spotted all over with orange-yellow; ribs covered with yellowish green scales forming five longitudinal streaks on each side; chin finely vermaculated with greyish brown; gular appendage very long and jet black. which extends across on to the front portion of the lateral wattles, the hinder half of which is pure white; belly and under parts dirty white, brown dotted; under side of wing-membranes dull brown tinged with yellowish green, the orange spots of upper surface being conspicuous.

Total length 9 inches.

Female.—Like the male; but the gular appendage is short, and black with white base.

Not uncommon in the neighbourhood of Kuching.

Total length 8½ inches.

Kuching, Sarawak *(E. Bartlett).*

32.—*Draco grandis*, N. Sp. S. M.

Habit, robust; head, large; limbs, short and thick; nostrils, directed outwards, tympanum large and naked; two large keeled scales directed backwards, on the top of the snout; two behind the eye; a series of round edged scales on each side of the mouth above the upper labials; scales of limbs, feeble keeled except along the hind edges; scales of belly, all keeled and sharp pointed; gular appendage, nearly as long as the head, covered with minute elongated scales, lateral wattles large.

Total length 10½ inches.

Bright reddish brown above, variegated with dark brown and greyish lines and marbling of black; interorbital space grey, behind which is a black W.; two elongated nuchal black blotches; wing-membranes greyish brown, with a series of longitudinal yellowish scales on the ribs, and three very faint bands across each; gular appendage, greyish white speckled with dirty brown; under parts, grey spotted and mottled with black; under

surface of wing-membranes, blueish white spotted with black.
Sarawak, Matang 800 feet (*E. Bartlett*).

33.—Aphaniotis fusca, Boulen. Cat. Lizards, vol. i, p. 274, 1885.

I have not observed this species yet. Sarawak (*Doria and Beccari*); Borneo (*Boulenger*).

34.—Gonyocephalus doriæ, Boulen. Cat. Lizards, vol. i, p. 284, 1885.

Rare. Sarawak (*Doria and Beccari*); Sarawak (*A. Everett*).

35.—Gonyocephalus liogaster, Boulen. Cat. Lizards, vol. i, p. 286, 1885. S. M.

Rare.
Borneo (*Doria, Bleeker and Wallace*); Kuching, Sarawak (*E. Bartlett*).

36.—Gonyocephalus miotympanum, Boulen. Cat. Lizards, vol. i, p. 287, 1885.

Borneo (*Günther*); Labuan (*Dillwyn*).

37.—Gonyocephalus borneensis, Boulen. Cat. Lizards, vol. i, 288, 1885.

Borneo (*Schlegel*); Sarawak (*Doria and Beccari*).

38.—Gonyocephalus grandis, Boulen. Cat. Lizards, vol. i, p. 298, 1885. S. M.

Matang, Sarawak (*Boulenger*); Mount Dulit (*C. Hose*) Penkalan Ampat, Sarawak (*G. D. Haviland*).

39.—Japalura nigrilabris, Boulen. Cat. Lizards, vol. i, p. 311, 1885. S. M.

Upper surface, reddish-brown tinged with green, variegated with yellowish white; a broad Y between the orbits black, in front and behind it deep chestnut; five blackish-brown wavy bands across the back with light spots in the centre of each, which gives them the appearance of W's, these band are much blacker on the sides; interspaces pale yellowish green varied with whitish scales, the first band is in front of the shoulder; legs marbled with brown; tail with broad brown bands; on the base of tail and loins there is a spear-shaped fold, the barb and shaft black, edged with yellowish buff; gular appendage straited with yellowish white, brown, and pinkish-red; lower part of throat and chest deep brick-red tinged with pink; belly and under-part of limbs yellowish white spotted and streaked with brown. Eye pale brown, pupil round and black with a gold ring.

Rare.

Sarawak (*Doria and Beccari*); Matang (*Boulenger*); Kuching (*E. Bartlett*).

40.—Calotes cristatellus, Boulen. Cat. Lizards, vol. i, p. 316, 1885. S. M.

The colours in this species are very variable; some are bright grass green without dark markings; another is tinged with blue with dark brown markings, while another greenish brown with darker marblings.

Not uncommon on hedges and in gardens; it is easily caught with the hand.

Borneo (*E. Belcher and Dillwyn*); Kina Balu (*G. D. Haviland*); Kuching (*E. Bartlett*).

41.—Lanthanotus borneensis, Boulen. Cat. Lizards, vol. xi, p. 302, 1885. S. M.

Very rare.

Sarawak (*Boulenger*); Rejang River, Sarawak (*C. A. Bampfylde*).

42.—Varanus Dumerilii, Boulen. Cat. Lizards, vol. xi, p. 312, 1885. S. M. Beyawak, Malays.

Not uncommon in gardens and jungle.

The largest in the collection is three feet.

Sarawak (*H. Low, Doria and Beccari*); Penkalan Ampat (*G. D. Haviland*); Baram and Mount Dulit (*C. Hose*); Kuching (*E. Bartlett*).

43.—Varanus heteropholis, Boulen. P. J. S., 1892., p. 506.

Rare.

Mount Dulit (*C. Hose*).

44.—Varanus rudicollis, Boulen. Cat. Lizards, vol. xi, p. 313, 1885. S. M.

Not common in the Kuching district.

One specimen measures three feet nine inches.

Sarawak (*Boulenger*); Baram River (*C. Hose*); Penkalan Ampat (*G. D. Haviland*).; Kuching and Matang (*E. Bartlett*).

45.—Varanus salvator, Boulen. Cat. Lizards, vol. ii, p. 314, 1885. S. M.

Not very common in the Kuching district. I have not met with very large specimens here; the largest we have are from Baram. Length 6 feet 8 inches; is the largest in the collection.

Borneo (*Dillwyn*); Sarawak (*H. Low, Doria and Beccari*); Sadong (*G. D. Haviland*); Baram (*C. Hose*); Mount Dulit (*C. Hose*); Kuching and Santubong (*E. Bartlett*).

46.—Tachydromus sexlineatus, Boulen. Cat. Lizards, vol. iii, p. 4, 1887. S. M.

This extraordinary and beautiful lizard is rather abundant in and about Kuching, frequenting grassy lanes and fields, or grassy gardens. It attains a length of 14 inches, the tail being more than 5 times the length of the body.

Sarawak (*Doria, Beccari and H. Low*); Borneo (*E. Belcher*); Matang (*Boulenger*); Matang and Kuching (*E. Bartlett*).

On the variation of the colours in the genera Mabuia and Lygosoma, with descriptions of new species.

During my residence here, I have had an opportunity of examining a very large series of nearly all the species of lizards found in Borneo, but *Mabuia* and *Lygosoma* being the most abundant, I am able to give more details of them, than of the other genera at present.

To make sure that my observations on the species are correct with regard to the markings and coloration, I have examined the various individuals for the purpose of determining the sex, and I think that these are most important points in ascertaining which assume the various colours during the breeding time (which appears very precarious) and in doing so I have found a variety of intermediate stages of markings and colours which are very deceptive, and liable to mislead one with regard to a species or even the sex, but having a large series of both sexes before me, it was much easier to settle.

In drawing up the descriptions I have selected some of the largest and most adult specimens of both sexes, and by the following short diagnosis of each sex they can be distinguished at once.

I may remark that all the characteristic beautiful colours of each species are lost in spirit specimens.

1. Mabuia Rugifera.

Male.—Tail, carinated to tip. Nearly black above; immaculate above and below. Throat, cobalt blue.

Female.—Above, blackish-brown; with pale brown longitudinal striations. Throat, green, black spotted.

2. Mabuia rubricollis, n. sp.

Male.—Tail, carinated to tip. Similar to *M. rugifera*. Throat, brick-red.

Female.—Similar to *M. rugifera*. Throat, vermilion.

3. Mabuia multifasiata.

Male adult.—Not polished above (dull); tail, perfectly smooth for half its length; not spotted on the sides of the body; a few rectangular white black sided spots on the sides of the base of the tail. Throat, chrome yellow.

Female adult.—Highly polished above; sides of body closely covered with white black sided rectangular spots from corner of mouth to base of tail. Throat, greyish white.

4. Mabuia rudis.

Male.—Not polished above (dull); tail, tri-bi-and unicarinated from base to tip; no white spots on the sides; a few yellow edged scales on the sides of the base of tail. Throat, blue.

Female.—Dull above; a yellowish white line from corner of mouth, which passes the shoulder and ends in yellowish white tipped scales in front of the hind leg. Throat, greenish-brown.

5. Mabuia Lewisi. n. sp.

Male adult.—Not polished above (dull); Tail, tri-bi-and unicarnated to the tip; no spots of white on the sides, a few white-tipped scales on the sides of the base of tail. Throat, orange red. Similar to *M. rudis*, but larger.

Female.—Like *M. rudis*, with line and spots, white not yellow. Throat, white.

47.—Euprepis belcheri, H. Low, Sarawak; Inh. and Prod. Appen. p. 411, 1848.

Mabuia Delalandi, Boulen. Cat. Lizards, vol. iii, p. 158, 1887.

A doubtful Bornean species.

The species is given in Low's list l. c., but it must be an error. The types in the British Museum are without a locality and presented by Sir E. Belcher; is it probable that these specimens were collected by H. Low and given to him?

48.—Mabuia rugifera, Boulen. Cat. Lizards, vol. iii, p. 184, 1887. S. M.

Male.—Upper part of head, sides of neck, dark bronze-green; rest of upper surface bright red-brown, finely vermaculated with black; chin and throat, pale cobalt blue with scattered yellow spots; chest, lemon yellow; rest of under parts deep vermilion red.

Mabuia rugifera.

Male.—Throat, pale cobalt blue, tinged with green on the chest and fore-limbs; belly, under-side of hind legs and tail, salmon pink.

Mabuia rugifera.

Male.—Above, blackish-brown, immaculate; chin and throat, bright grass-green; belly bent and under-side of tail, salmon-red.

Obtained June, 1893, near Kuching.

Mabuia rugifera.

Male.—Above, blackish-brown, immaculate; eye-lids, upper and lower lips, chin, throat and upper part of chest, lemon yellow; belly and under part of tail, salmon red.

Two males procured Nov., 1893, are marked and the colours are exactly alike.

Mabuia rugifera.

Female.—Above dark brown, streaked with yellowish brown, from superciliary line and corner of mouth to base of tail; lips, chin and throat, pale blue, tinged with green; nearly all the scales have a black terminal band, these black bands are irregular and give the throat a variegated appearance; chest, yellowish green; belly and under part of tail, pinkish salmon.

Obtained October 13, 1893.

Mabuia rugifera.

Female.—Chin and throat, yellowish green, spotted with black; belly, under-side of hind-limbs, reddish salmon tinged with greenish blue; under side of tail, reddish salmon.

Obtained September, 1893.

This beautiful little species is rather abundant near Kuching. I have had an opportunity of examining a very fine series of males and females; in the adults the colours are very brilliant.

They inhabit the sandy paths in the jungle.

All the species of *Mabuia* and *Tygosoma*, are called by the Malays Bĕnkároug.

Matang, Borneo (*Boulenger*); Sarawak (*Doria* and *Beccari*) Kuching, Sarawak (*E. Bartlett*).

49.—Mabuia rubricollis, n. sp.? S. M.

Male.—Similar to *M. rugifera*. Above, blackish brown; upper and lower lips, orange-red fading off on the sides of the neck; chin and throat, lemon yellow; chest and rest of under parts, tinged with salmon pink.

Mabuia rubricollis, n. sp.

Male.—Above blackish-brown; lips, chin and throat vermilion red; rest of under parts, salmon pink.

Obtained October 27, 1893.

Mabuia rubricollis, n. sp.

Female.—Above, dark brown, or blackish, streaked and spotted with bright red-brown; lips, chin, throat and chest, brick-red, brightest on the chin; rest of under parts, salmon pink.

Mabuia rubricollis, n. sp.

Female.—Superciliary streak, lips chin and throat, bright vermilion red; belly, pinkish tinged with green; under parts of tail, pale salmon pink.

Have separated this form from *M. rugifera* on account of its brilliant red throat, whereas in *M. rugifera* in the adult it is pale cobalt blue, otherwise the two lizards are similar, but at the same time we obtain males and females of the two species constantly in the same district, therefore, we may consider it a local race or a district species, especially when we look at the three species of *Halcyon* given by Mr. R. B. Sharpe in the British Museum Catalague.

This lizard is certainly not so abundant as *M. rugifera*, although it inhabits the same sandy lanes and jungle paths about Kuching, and the district.

I have examined the sexes of a large series.

Kuching, Sarawak (*E. Bartlett.*)

50.—*Mabuia multifasciata*, Boulen. Cat. Lizards, vol. iii, p. 186, 1887. S.M.

Male.—Sides, unspotted; upper and lower lips, brick red; chin and throat, chrome yellow; belly, dark grey tinged with green; under part of tail, pale brown.

Obtained October, 1893.

This is an adult male in breeding colours, and many have the sides of the neck brick-red.

Mabuia multifasciata.

Male.—Dorso-lateral band, bright-red; upper and lower lips, brick-red; chin and throat, greyish-white speckled with yellow; belly, pale yellowish-brown.

A young male assuming the yellow throat.

Mabuia multifasciata.

Male.—Above, dark brown; dorsolateral line, pale brownish-buff; sides, dark-brown, unspotted; chin and throat, grey; lips, tinged with brick red; chest and belly, dull green; under part of tail, silvery white.

A young male.

Mabuia multifasciata.

Female.—Above, dark-brown, with five longitudinal black lines; dorso-lateral streak, pale brown; sides, blackish-brown; a series of yellowish white spots from the ear along the sides to the base of tail; chin and throat, silvery white; chest belly and underside of tail, yellowish-brown.

Old female in breeding colours.

Mabuia multifasciata.

Female.—Above, dark-brown, and iridescent; sides below the dorso-lateral streak, brown tinged with bright vermilion-red, and spotted with yellowish-white; throat, greyish-white; belly, yellowish brown.

Obtained September 21, 1893.

Young female.

The average length of this species is from 10 to 12 inches.

This is the most abundant species in Sarawak; it is found on the trunks of felled trees and on the ground in every road and path throughout the country. I have carefully examined hundreds of them and find a great variety of colours in the males, some with metallic green and red bands on the sides of the neck, while others are brilliant, brick-red on the sides of the neck, and above the shoulders; at the same time they are easily distinguished from all the other males by the smooth terminal half or two-thirds of the tail.

Sarawak, (*H. Low, Doria and Beccari*); Kuching Sarawak, (*E. Bartlett*), Borneo, (*Cantor*).

51.—*Mabuia rudis*, Boulen., Cat. Lizards, vol. iii, p. 188.
1887. S. M.

Male.—Above, dark greenish-brown with four longitudinal rows of blackish spots; dorso-lateral streak, pale greenish-brown; sides, red-brown variegated with black from ear to base of tail; upper surface of legs, red-brown; chin, throat, and sides of neck, bright cobalt blue; chest, belly and under-parts, grass-green; scales of vent and under part of tail, silvery-white.

Mabuia rudis.

Male.—Above, rich red-brown; dorso-lateral streak, yellowish brown; sides, rich brown tinged with vermilion, each scale edged with black; upper surface of legs, like the back; a bright green stripe from the ear to the shoulder, which is gradually lost on the sides of the body; chin, throat and chest, greenish blue variously speckled with orange-yellow; belly, sides of same, and under part of fore limbs, pale vermilion-red tinged with green, the latter colour brightest on the abdomen and hind-legs; scales of vent and underpart of tail, silvery-white.

Obtained Sept. 19, 1893.

Mabuia rudis.

Male.—Sides, unspotted; upper and lower lips, chin, throat, and fore part of chest, pale blue, much speckled with black; chest and belly, grass-green; under part of hind limbs and tail brown.

Obtained November 2, 1893.

Mabuia rudis.

Male.—Sides, unspotted; chin and throat, cobalt blue with a few scattered orange-yellow and black spots; chest and rest of under parts, grass-green.

Obtained October 26, 1893.

Mabuia rudis.

Female.—Above, chocolate-brown, with four longitudinal rows of black spots, some confluent; a well defined light dorso-lateral streak; sides, blackish; a yellow line from the corner of the mouth passes over the shoulder and terminates in blackish yellow-edged spots on the sides of the tail; fore limbs, brown with black yellow-edged spots on the hinder surface; throat and belly, greenish-brown.

Obtained August 30, 1893.

Mabuia rudis.

Female.—Above, brown; sides, nearly black; streak from corner of mouth to beyond the shoulder, greenish yellow; chin, throat, and chest, pale grass-green; belly and under parts, light-brown faintly tinged with green.

Sept. 21, 1893.

Mabuia rudis

Female.—Above, red-brown, with five distinct black longitudinal dorsal streaks; dorso-lateral line, pale-brown; sides, blackish brown; from the corner of the mouth a bright yellow streak which passes over the fore arm and ends in yellow spots in front of the hind leg, also a few yellowish spots on the sides of the base of the tail; chin, throat, and belly, dark greenish-brown.

Mabuia rudis.

Female.—Sides, yellow spotted from the cheeks to hind legs, with a few chrome yellow spots on the neck, on a line with the ear; without the usual white line from corner of mouth; chin and throat, greyish white; chest and rest of underparts, dull-brown tinged with yellow.

Obtained October 26, 1893.

The average length of adults of this species is from eight to ten inches.

Plentiful, but not so common as *M. multifasciata.*

I have described the colours of several individuals which are very brilliant when alive. This lizard is easily distinguished from all the others, being very robust in habit, the tail is carinated to the tip, and very dark-brown, almost black above.

Matang and Kuching, Sarawak. (*E. Bartlett*).

52.—Mabuia rudis, var. Kuchingensis, n. sp. S. M.

Female.—Above, dark brown; dorso-lateral band, nearly black; sides of neck and body to base of tail, closely barred with bright chrome yellow-edged black spots; chin and throat, greyish white; chest and rest of under parts, dull brown tinged with yellow.

This specimen is so distinctly marked and readily distinguished from the true *M. rudis.* I considered it worth separating for the present. Almost appears like a hybrid.

Kuching (*E. Bartlett*).

53.—Mabuia Lewisi, n. sp. S. M.

Male.—Habit, robust. Above, dark brown; dorso-lateral streak, pale brown; sides, dark-green unspotted; upper and lower lips, chin, throat, chest, and sides of neck, rich orange red; under part of fore arms, and belly, bright lemon-yellow; scales of vent and under part of tail, pure silvery-white.

Mabuia Lewisi n. sp.

Female.—Above, brown paler than the male; dorso-lateral stripe, pale brown; sides of body, dark brown; a buff coloured streak from the corner of the mouth to hind limb; chin and throat, white; belly, yellowish-green; under sides of limbs and tail, pale greenish-brown.

Similar to *Mabuia rudis,* but the carinations are not so bold, and the points do not overlap like those of *M. rudis.* It is without the four or five longitudinal rows of small black specks on the back, which is always present in *M. rudis;* and easily distinguished when alive by its bright-red throat and other colours.

This fine species I procured on Santubong at about 200ft., others near Kuching. I have much pleasure in naming it after M. J. E. A. Lewis, who always takes much interest, and does a great deal towards increasing the collection, besides rendering me valuable assistance respecting the particulars of the specimens.

54.—*Mabuia saravacensis*, n. sp. S. M.

Habit, robust; head, broad behind; scales, twenty-eight round the body; back, nearly the whole length of tail and upper surface of fore limbs, tricarinate; hind limbs above, bi- and tricarinate; under parts, smooth.

Above, pale dull-brown, with irregular transverse bars of black yellow and white-edged spots, which pass over on to the sides of the belly; two distinct round black spots on the parietals; eyelids, yellow; whole of underparts, bright grass-green.

Rare in this locality.

Santubong and Kuching (*E. Bartlett*).

55.—*Lygosoma variegatum*, Boulen. Cat. Lizards, iii, p. 246, 1887. S. M.

Male.—Above, dull brown; marbled, and with two longitudinal rows of unequal sized spots down the back; chin, throat, and breast, deep cobalt blue; paler blue on the chest and belly; under sides of fore arms, vent and hind legs, dirty yellow; under surface of tail, french grey, or bluish grey.

Lygosoma variegatum.

Female.—Above, like the male; chin, and throat, whitish; whole of under parts including limbs, bright yellow; under side of tail, bluish-grey.

She is the most beautiful of all the lizards found here. In old males, the cobalt blue of the throat is very brilliant.

It is not very abundant.

Borneo (*L. L. Dillwyn*) Kuching, Sarawak (*E. Bartlett*).

56.—*Lygosoma kinabaluensis*, n. sp. S. M.

Male.—Similar to *L. variegatum*, but the back is mottled and without striations, and without a distinct dorsolateral band.

This small species is quite distinct, therefore, I name it to distinguish it from the others at present, until I can procure more specimens.

Being a spirit specimen, I am unable to give the decided colours. Kina Balu, N. Borneo (*G. D. Haviland.*)

57.—*Lygosoma olivaceum*, Boulen., Cat. Lizards, vol. iiii, p. 251, 1887. S. M.

Back buff, with nine pale interrupted bands across the back; hind legs, barred like the back; a buff band above the hind leg; chin and throat, yellowish green; rest of under parts, grass-green, tinged with blue.

This appears to be a very scarce species in the district, having only procured two specimens.

Borneo *(A. R. Wallace)*; Sarawak *(A. Everet)*; Kuching. *(E. Bartlett)*.

58.—*Lygosoma vittatum*, Boulen., Cat. Lizards, vol. iii, p. 252, 1887. The Verandah Lizard, S. M.

Male and Female.—Above, black, variegated with buff speckles; a greenish white streak between the eyes; a greenish white superciliary streak which extends beyond the shoulder and fades away on the back; another greenish white-streak from tip of snout passes under the eye and fades away beyond the shoulder; lower lips, green black-spotted; chin, throat, and belly, bright grass-green, tinged with blue on the throat. Sexes alike. This very pretty and active lizard is to be found in nearly all the jungle houses and especially about the verandahs, picking up ants, and various insects which are always numerous in these places.

Borneo *(L. L. Dillwyn)*; Sarawak *(Doria and Beccari)*; Rejang River *(C. A. Bampfylde)*; Santubong and Kuching, *(E. Bartlett)*.

59.—*Lygosoma nitens*, Boulen., Cat. Lizards, vol. iii, p. 262, 1887. S. M.

Very rare in this district.

Sarawak *(Doria and Beccari)*; Kuching *(E. Bartlett)*.

60.—*Lygosoma parietale*, Boulen., Cat. Lizards, vol. iii, p. 299, 1887. S. M.

Male and Female.—Above, grey tinged with green; under parts, pale yellowish buff.

I cannot detect any variation in the colour of the sexes of this species. It is tolerably common on the sea shore.

Sarawak *(Doria and Beccari)*; Santubong and Kuching *(E. Bartlett)*.

61.—Lygosoma (Riopa) Bampfyldei, n. sp. S. M.

Habit, stout; limbs, short and thick; scales, all smooth; six upper and six lower labials; ten small preanals.

Pale brown, above and below, immaculate; with a dark brown patch on the front part of the head, another on the crown and hind neck, divided from the former by a pale band from eye to eye; upper surface of limbs and tail dusky brown.

Rejang River, Sarawak (*C. A. Bampfylde*).

62.—Tropidophorus Beccari, Boulen., Cat. Lizards, vol. iii, p. 360, 1887. Beccari's Lizard.

Sarawak (*Doria and Beccari*); Matang (*G. A. Boulenger*).

63.—Tropidophorus Brookii, Boulen., Cat. Lizards, vol. iii, p. 361, 1887. The Raja's Lizard, S. M.

Upper and lower lips, red-brown; under parts, white,

Sarawak (*H. Low*); Sarawak (*E. Belcher*); Santubong and Kuching (*E. Bartlett*).

On a New Species of "Philentoma."

By EDWARD BARTLETT,

Curator of the Sarawak Museum.

1.—Philentoma velatum, Blyth. *Adult male.*—General colour, bright greyish blue; face and part of the throat, black; lower part of throat and breast, maroon.

2.—Philentoma pyrrhopterum., Blyth. *Adult male.*—Head, neck, mantle, lesser wing-coverts, chin, throat, and sides of breast, greyish-blue; greater wing-coverts, secondaries and tail chestnut; primaries, dusky brown; under-parts, dirty white; thighs, blue.

3.—Philentoma Maxwelli, n. sp.

Adult male.—Similar to *P. pyrrhopterum*, but with a dark chestnut patch on the middle of the breast; the blue of the head and neck much brighter; the chestnut of the wing-coverts secondaries and tail, much darker and richer; some of the outer webs of the inner primaries also chestnut; under-parts much purer white; thighs buff, not blue like those of *P. pyrrhopterum*.

This species was obtained in the jungle not far from Kuching.

In describing this new bird, I considered it advisable to give a short diagnosis of the two older and well known forms, of which this museum contains a fine series.

In referring to Mr. Sharpe's description of *P. pyrrhopterum*, (vol. iv., p. 365), I find that he says the " wings and tail, chestnut" in the young male, but at page 366, he states that " the quills and tail-feathers are dusky blackish on the inner web, greyish blue externally "! I have examined all our specimens carefully and cannot find a trace of the latter colours on the tail-feathers; and certainly no greyish blue on the primaries.

I have much pleasure in naming this new species after the Hon'ble F. R. O. Maxwell, Resident of Sarawak.